PRACTICAL NLP
APPLICATIONS

Tim Brunson, PhD

The International Hypnosis Research Institute, LLC

CONTENTS

INTRODUCTION

NLP techniques and interventions are widely used by numerous qualified and a high number of minimally trained practitioners throughout the world. The techniques are normally simple enough that a relative novice can achieve startling results. Tony Robbins, the extremely successful self-help speaker and author, started doing rapid phobia cures over the radio shortly after he was introduced to NLP by John Grinder. Robbins is not a certified practitioner even though he has successfully used NLP-like techniques to help thousands of people.

Over the past decade NLP notables have added physical health as a valid application. So at this point, NLP is generally considered appropriate for mental health, medicine, coaching, business applications, and self-help.

MENTAL HEALTH

A study of NLP history reveals that it originated as a mental health or psychology technique. As mentioned in *Mastering the NLP Communication Model*, the early influences were several therapists and a psychiatrist. Therefore, its techniques provide the properly licensed practitioner an arsenal of simple and effective tools. It can be effectively used for the treatment of addictions, anxiety and stress, and to address fears and phobias.

The reason that this is possible can be attributed back to the NLP Communication Model. Most mental disorders center on anxiety and stress or fears and phobias. These conditions are states, which are closely related to internal representations and filters. Therefore, they present ideal opportunities for the qualified NLP Practitioner.

Please note that the reason that I mention the necessity of being qualified is that should a certified Practitioner or someone who has acquired a few NLP skills begin addressing mental disorders without the proper

When I relate NLP to self-improvement and self-actualization, I am referring to the last two levels and relegating the others to the physical and mental health arenas. Therefore, I am focusing on topics such as self-esteem, confidence, achievement, respect for oneself and others, problem solving, creativity and intuition.

Now that I have clarified this issue, it is appropriate to point out that the subject who is seeking to use NLP interventions desires to move from their current status quo state to what they feel represents their true potential. I include here things as mundane as improving reading speed, enhancing musical performance, and lowering a golf handicap. What is getting in the way is typically limiting filters. Therefore, many of the techniques that are used for mental health applications would work here as well.

The Practitioner should elicit beliefs, values, and meta-programs to help discern blockages and limitations. In the last book in this series I discussed how calibrating to a subject's meta-programs occurs in modeling. The same technique is valid here as well. You should also be on the lookout for conflicting beliefs and negative anchors. When the former occurs a parts-integration technique would be in order. For the latter, I would use a collapsing anchor intervention. Let me explain collapsing anchors more in detail.

An anchor is a perception that triggers a specific state. This can occur within any one of the five modalities. A smell can inspire the memory of your mother if it reminds you of her favorite perfume. Likewise, if someone touches you on the shoulder while grieving at a funeral and later in the day someone else touches you in the same spot, the grieving state will again be felt. This is called firing an anchor.

Anchors can be installed on purpose. If your subject is experiencing a state, a word, touch, smell, or something they see can become inadvertently related. As a Practitioner you are doing this on purpose.

Here is an example. Suppose a person becomes overly tense before studying for an exam. You ask them to think about the last time that this happened. While they are recalling it, as soon as they are in what you feel is a peak state, you say a word or perhaps lightly touch them on their right wrist.

Next break the state by asking a neutral question. You may then test your anchor by firing it to see if you elicit the same state.

Once you have tested it and again break the state,

ask your subject to think of a time when they felt particularly empowered, confident, and relaxed. Once they are in a peak state, touch them on the left wrist. Then release your anchor and again ask a neutral question to break the state.

Next ask them to again think of the anxiety associated with studying, touch them on the right wrist, which creates the appropriate anchor. Then almost immediately touch them on their other wrist, which is their positive anchor. In a few seconds, release the negative anchor and watch their state change right before your eyes. What you have done is collapsed their negative anchor and de-programmed their limiting filter.

This is an example of an extremely simple technique for self-improvement. Of course, in this example I was illustrating a situation where a subject was working with a Practitioner. The second person is not always necessary. This is a technique that someone can do without any assistance.

NLP FOR COACHING

NLP is increasingly used by life coaches as well as sports coaches. The intent is to focus on the achievement of the subject regarding goals or specific skills. Again, filters are generally the problem that is going to be addressed. Goals and skills correlate to internal representations and mental states. Filters control their manifestation. Therefore, change the filter, change the representation and state.

Many of the techniques used for mental health applications will work here as well. However, the great thing about NLP for coaching is that if you are not working with mental disorders that are the subject of mental health laws, there is a wide range of opportunities available for the aspiring NLP Practitioner. I have colleagues who have used their NLP training to work with children who are attempting to do better in school, as well as with highly paid professional athletes.

The collapsing anchor technique just described is an excellent one to use when limiting beliefs seem to be the problem. Helping a quarterback improve his passing game could very well be an example where this could be used. I also like the various timeline techniques that are used by Practitioners. For instance, you may establish a physical timeline in a hallway, get the subject to move back to a point where they remember peak performance, and create an anchor such as a specific keyword.

Then have them move forward in time to the next time when they need to perform the same task. Once they are in that position, fire the anchor and again notice the change in their physiology. This is a very simple technique that can be used in a coaching situation.

NLP FOR BUSINESS APPLICATIONS

Another form of coaching is done by consultants who use NLP to help business managers and owners. Techniques such as the Disney Strategy can help with creativity issues. The timeline example just discussed can be used when limiting beliefs concerning the future of a business is an issue.

There are also a wide range of techniques that can be used to enhance business communication, to include the sales process and leadership. By understanding NLP theory, you can more easily understand how your employers, suppliers, and customers or clients communicate and think. Each one of them will understand your verbal and written communication once they have processed them through their filters. When you learn to recognize their values, beliefs, and meta-programs, you will have the opportunity to communicate with them in the language with which they feel more comfortable.

This is just another example of how to use rapport in these situations. Of course, the rapport skills that I discussed in *Developing Instant Rapport* most definitely apply here as well. Additionally, when you realize the importance of anchoring states, you can recognize the value of all communication regarding the promotion of ideas, products, and services. Therefore, a knowledgeable NLP Practitioner, whether it is a consultant, trainer, or the manager/owner, will have the opportunity to alter anchors or meta-programs so that they can become more successful.

NLP FOR MEDICINE

The application of NLP interventions in medicine and physical health is a relatively new category. Its development has paralleled interest in mind/body health, which is often referred to as integrative health or medicine, complementary medicine, or alternative medicine.

The premise here is that all physical conditions are related to mental states. Therefore, internal representations and filters would be significant as well. For instance, if someone has cancer, they see themselves as a cancer patient. This is an internal representation. It is also very closely related to both their state and their filters. A lady, who had 16 tumors in her mouth, once told me that she believed that her mind was so powerful that it made her sick. Her meta-programs were that of a victim, which includes self-sorting and away from motivation. I asked her if she was convinced that her mind was actually that powerful. She immediately and emotionally responded in the affirmative. I then suggested that if her mind was that powerful, perhaps she would allow it to heal her body. She suddenly gave me a puzzled look. I had just implied that she could change her meta-programs to empowerment and toward-motivation. A few months later she called to proudly inform me that her cancer was in total remission.

I've also successfully used NLP for allergy elimination. Ann King, a talented hypnotherapist who practices in Texas, has an effective NLP technique for allergy elimination that has helped hundreds of people who have had recurring allergy problems.

Although NLP for health issues is somewhat more controversial than other applications and needs considerable scientific validation, I find that it is very similar in concept to several of the ideas that I use in the ANNH and Neurology of Suggestion courses. As these are based on firm scientific research, they lend considerable credibility to the cases discussed by many of the more innovative NLP authors.

DEMONSTRATION

1

I want you to think of three times or events in your past. The first one should be a time when you felt extremely healthy. This should be a time when your breathing, movement, and energy were at their peak. As you remember that time, try to see it through your eyes, hear it through your ears, and sense how you felt. While holding onto this feeling of complete health, think of another time when you were extremely happy. This could be a time when you were with people who were special to you or an important event that brought you lots of joy. Again, see, hear, and feel it through your eyes, ears, and body as vividly as you can. Hold on to this thought. Now think of another time when you felt empowered as you just completed an important task that symbolized a milestone in your life. This could be as simple as cleaning the garage or kitchen, or even graduation from a school or program, or the accomplishment of some great adventure. Once again, make this memory as associated and vivid as you can. Now while holding on to these combined feelings of fantastic health, happiness, and accomplishment, imagine that you have hired someone to write a theme song or melody for you. This could be something very original or possibly even a favorite song or music from your past. Allow that music to play in your mind as you again relive that time of perfect health, happiness, and accomplishment. Imagine that you are absorbing the vibration of the music, feeling and seeing any colors associated with that wonderful state. Hold on to that state as long as you would like to.

Now as you listen to my voice, ponder why this exercise created this state. Think about it. Understand it intellectually. Realize that you have created a resource that you now wish to test. And to test it, think of an event that you anticipate happening in the future. This may be a time when you know that you are going to be challenged. It may be a time when you know that you need to perform at your best. Or perhaps it could be a time when you know that you need to be strong. As you think of this time, allow your mind to start playing your song. This is the song that you anchored to your events of perfect wellness, happiness, and self-accomplishment. Notice how your feelings begin to change. Notice how you are empowered and capable of making better choices in life.

THE FUTURE OF NLP

While many aspects of Neuro-Linguistic Programming are timeless, in many ways the field is becoming increasingly obsolete as new discoveries are being made in how the brain and mind work. This chapter will talk about the state of the field, the value of learning NLP, and where I think it is going.

NLP is a somewhat controversial yet very effective field of psychology. Some would say that psychology did not need yet another school of thought. Already it had Freudian psychoanalysis – which a field that has increasingly achieving disfavor among the professionals – Jungian psychology, Gestalt Therapy, and a slew of rapid techniques and other theories. Those who are intellectually and emotionally wedded to their favorite theories have had considerable discomfort with NLP. Yet, even they cannot argue or explain countless examples of the successful applications of NLP.

The attractiveness of NLP can also be found in its pervasiveness. As pointed out in the previous chapters, there are plenty of techniques available to professionals in the medical and psychology fields, as well as many that can be easily mastered by coaches, consultants, and laymen and women who are interested in self-help applications. All of these are based upon a central NLP Communication Model.

Another key feature is that NLP tends to be more scientifically relevant. When it was developed it was influenced by Gestalt Therapy - which was a significant development in the world of psychology - and Dr. Erickson's unique approach to hypnotherapy. Its development paralleled many of the innovations in computer science that were part of the revolution in cognitive studies that we call the Information Age. This lent it the more algorithmic attributes that were missing in traditional psychotherapy.

The congruence of NLP with ANNH theories is no mistake. Likewise, both fields are influenced by the other cognitive sciences. However, NLP has not significantly evolved much since the post-Grinder and Bandler generation of authors – such as Robert Dilts – added significant additional concepts and techniques. (Chief among these was the logical levels idea and meta-programs.) Innovations and recent discoveries in neurology, neurofeedback, and artificial intelligence are better represented in ANNH than they are in NLP. NLP authors and instructors largely focus on teaching the classical approaches advocated by the first couple of generations. Nevertheless, I still see a great value in pursuing formal NLP Practitioner and Master Practitioner training

NLP TRAINING AND CERTIFICATIONS

There are two basic NLP certifications. These are the Practitioner and Master Practitioner Levels. Most organizations – many of which have disappeared – that ever claimed to be credentialing authorities for NLP certifications have generally agreed that it required 130 hours of instruction for each of these programs. The way that they were most often presented was in the form of 16 hours per month, a process that normally took around eight to nine months to complete. Many of the programs required a practical test – which was sometimes called an integration – where the student are required to demonstrate their skills. Some programs require a written examination as well.

There has been a trend toward compacting NLP certifications into comprehensive programs that last ten days or less. These are normally preceded by a self-study book that must be completed – and test passed – before the ten-day marathon training begins.

My formal training was received in the longer, two-year format. While I may be partial to that format due my familiarity, I think that it is more productive and produces superior practitioners. The reason for this conclusion is that much of the integration of NLP theory and practice comes from the ability to observe real live communication. Learning theory and techniques during a 16-hour weekend and then completing assignments during the intervening month provides the student with an increased ability to absorb and integrate the lessons. Unfortunately, this format may dissuade many potential students who want to progress at a much more rapid pace. Also, sometimes the accelerated formats can be presented at a significantly lower cost while providing a substantially higher profit for the trainers.

Some Master Practitioners may be interested in becoming certified instructors. The program that I went through was conducted by John Overdurf and Julie Silverthorne, who were co-trainers and assistants for Richard Bandler. Their program, which I believe mirrors those offered by Bandler and Tad James, requires two weeks of intensive instructor training, a very rigorous written exam, and a week of demonstrations where the student displays their ability to teach the material. (I must point out that when I went through the program all the material was based upon content that was 30 to 40 years old.)

NLP ORGANIZATIONS

The problem with NLP certification is the lack of consistent agreement of its regulation. This requires the existence and consistency of peer organizations. The International Association of NLP, the American Board of NLP, Association for Neuro-Linguistic Programming, and the International Association of NLP-Institutes are just a few of the organizations that have claimed or currently claim to regulate the field. Note that these organizations assure that practitioners adhere to established standards – most of which are based upon theory that is decades old. This should not be surprising, as this problem is the same as is experienced by just about every reputable trade and professional organization. Their attempt to protect the purity of their dogma has the side effect of assuring mediocrity and obsolescence.

CURRENT OR OBSOLETE?

Any field or discipline is relevant until it is not. This is true both for NLP and ANNH. The NLP Communication Model, which is the foundation of the field, consists of an approach that is still congruent with much of which has been revealed within the areas of neurology, artificial intelligence, and quantum physics – which incidentally are the three pillars of ANNH. Many NLP core concepts, such as the NLP Communication Model, are timeless. Their enduring value should be emphasized and studied further until they are replaced by something more current.

NLP theorists commit the same sins as others in medicine and psychology. Findings based upon evidence, correlations, and case studies may lead to empirical conclusions that certain results are predictable. The flaw here is that the etiology – meaning causation – is missing. What this means is that claims are being made that are totally devoid of any understanding or relevant theory as to why they occur. This opens up opportunities for logical fallacies to occur as well as potentially prevent or retard subsequent intellectual evolution. ANNH is intended to rectify this. However, I doubt that my comments will ever impact how NLP training is conducted – although I feel that there is a significant opportunity to explain why the techniques work.

INTEGRATING NLP INTO YOUR PERSONAL LIFE

What I have attempted to do in this book is to explain NLP to the uninitiated as well as clarify its essence to those who have had previous exposure and training in the field. If you consider the simplicity and elegance of the NLP Communication Model, this is actually not very difficult. It all comes down to one simple concept. Your filters affect your internal representations, your state, and behavior. As your filters control your perception of reality, then by changing them your reality changes. I can't get more simplistic than that.

So then what is reality? This is not a question that NLP authors traditionally address. However, I do remember a phrase that is used constantly by American Pacific University president, Matthew James, PhD. He said that no matter what or who you think you are, you are much more than that.

While I don't consider Matt James a quantum scientist, his statement mirrors the quantum proposition that the universe is full of endless possibilities and potentials, which are affected by our limiting filters. When I read this I immediately thought of the NLP Communication Model filters. Frankly, I don't see much difference. Filters create our sense of reality. However, the reality that results is more of a convenient illusion. Therefore, when it comes to mental health and happiness, physical health, and self-actualization, our current sense of reality is merely a choice. This is a choice that includes a responsibility to choose. If you don't like your reality, then NLP techniques give you an elegant way of finding a new one.

As Robert Dilts frequently wrote, a lot of our happiness and therefore our ability to access these endless realities comes from the realization that we operate at multiple levels. These are environment, behaviors, capabilities/strategies, beliefs and values, identity/mission, and spirituality/purpose. For the sake of argument, suppose that the NLP Communication Model exists at each one of these levels. Each of them has their own unique filters that result in a different set of internal representations and states.

The problem that Dilts reminds us of is the need for congruence to occur between these levels. For instance, is your current behavior congruent with your self-identity and/or your mission in life? If not, a feeling of discomfort occurs. Although I am oversimplifying Dilt's theory, I hope that you get the point. Our filters affect our states and behavior, but do so at multiple levels simultaneously. Another way of looking at this is by realizing the various roles that you play. For instance, I am a hypnotherapist, cognitive scientist, father, husband, etc. The question is whether I am congruent in all of these roles. If not, there is a need for transformation.

When deciding whether you have the opportunity to apply NLP in your life, the first thing that you need to explore is whether there is a feeling of dissonance. If so, it is appropriate to do some self-discovery as you explore or calibrate to you own state, internal representations, and especially explore your filters. You must understand your beliefs, values, and meta-programs. If your life is happy and harmonious, you most likely don't have the need or desire to change. In other words, don't screw with happiness. On the other hand, if you have a nagging feeling of emotional or physical discomfort, then you may wish to pursue a conscious program for change. In that case, here are some questions that you may wish to ask yourself:

1) Who am I? Am I a "noun" or a "verb?" Am I an ever evolving piece of art or someone who is leading an automatic, programmed existence? Re-

member Matt James' statement that you are much more than you think you are. By the way it is always easier to change if you see yourself as a verb rather than as a noun.

2)   What are my beliefs? Where did they come from? Are they indoctrinated and programmed? Or, did I choose them after a rational analysis? Am I a captive of my beliefs or can I change them when I choose?

3)   Am I always reacting to situations in my life or do I always seek to make things happen for me and those who I care about?

4)   Am I motivated primarily to avoid pain and suffering? Or, am I motivated by my desire to achieve my goals?

5)   Do I find myself always talking about "me" and otherwise incessantly attempting to validate myself by reminding people around me about my accomplishments and beliefs? Or, do I spend my time caring for others and being concerned how they feel? (Being careful, of course, not to equate this with the dysfunctional role of a co-dependent.)

6)   Do I connect easily and well with others? If so, do they feel better once they are in my presence?

Your answers to these questions can tell you a lot about your current status. They may also give you valuable information about your opportunities to change. If you are never in rapport with others, try improving your rapport skills. If you are incessantly insisting on always being the "life of the party" and always boasting about your accomplishments and opinions, try becoming a better listener and showing a sincere interest in others. Do this and see how your life can easily change.

Additionally, self-applying NLP techniques can also be extremely helpful. Make a list of all the times in your life when you were successful and resourceful. Walk your timeline back to that point and anchor that resource. Next move forward along your timeline to a future challenge, fire your anchor and watch your fears fade easily and quickly. Learn to deprogram your negative and unresourceful feelings and constantly trigger your happier resources. NLP contains a wide range of skills designed to change your filters so that your internal representations and emotional state allow you to create a more desirable version of you.

Although NLP has often been thought of as a rather overwhelming collection of techniques, the way I have presented it I hope that you now see it is a rather elegant and surprisingly simple, yet powerful concept. Simply, change your filters and change your reality. If you take nothing but that idea from this book, you have been very successful. If you are inspired to receive more NLP training, I wish you the best.

DEMONSTRATION 2

This is an exercise in which you assess your current situation, discover one or more things that you would like to change about how you think and communicate, and setting up NLP-oriented protocols for change. You may wish to use a pen and paper to record your thoughts and ideas.

First start by considering your current situation. The following questions may help you in this process.

Who am I? Am I a "noun" or a "verb?" Am I an ever evolving piece of art or someone who is leading an automatic, programmed existence? Remember Matt James' statement that you are much more than you think you are. By the way it is always easier to change if you see yourself as a verb rather than as a noun.

What are my beliefs? Where did they come from?

Are they indoctrinated and programmed? Or, did I choose them after a rational analysis? Am I a captive of my beliefs or can I change them when I choose?

Am I always reacting to situations in my life or do I always seek to make things happen for me and those who I care about?

Am I motivated primarily to avoid pain and suffering? Or, am I motivated by my desire to achieve my goals?

Do I find myself always talking about "me" and otherwise incessantly attempting to validate myself by reminding people around me about my accomplishments and beliefs? Or, do I spend my time caring for others and being concerned how they feel? (Being careful, of course, not to equate this with the dysfunctional role of a co-dependent.)

Do I connect easily and well with others? If so, do they feel better once they are in my presence?

After you've taken plenty of time to consider your current situation, think of one or two areas of your life that you want to improve. For instance, if you find that you have a difficulty reaching goals or forming strong relationships, you may want to explore your beliefs, values, and the Meta-Programs, which are the various psychological filters that you use when you perceive your environment. Some people find it useful to discuss the previously presented questions with a friend. Objective input from a clinician or a trusted friend may give you a meaningful perspective that you had not considered.

Once you obtain your list of desired changes, it is then time to come up with a transformative plan. Of course, merely asking the questions may be sufficient as a change intervention. Self-awareness is very powerful. Otherwise, sitting down, relaxing, and thinking of a time when you did not have that problem or that you found your performance was at its peak level will help you gather resources that you can apply now and in the future. If you find that your values, beliefs, and other filters are resulting in less than total happiness and satisfaction, then intentionally deciding to replace these filters through either reframing or rehearsing alternatives will most definitely help. Remember that changing your filters affects your internal representations, mental states, and behaviors.

ABOUT THE AUTHOR

This series is by Tim Brunson, who holds both Doctor of Clinical Hypnotherapy and Doctor of Philosophy Clinical Hypnotherapy degrees, has practiced hypnotherapy for 29 years with clients and patients referred to him by medical and mental health practitioners, has trained clinicians internationally, and has almost 3,000 hours of training much of which was medical and mental health related. Many of his courses are already available through Amazon in either short-read or longer books.

RESOURCES

General:

The International Hypnosis Research Institute

IHRI membership

Advanced-Neuro-Noetic-Hypnosis

Courses

Books, E-Books, And Audiobooks:

Sets

Elman Hypnotherapy: Beyond the Basics

Improving Your Performance Genius

Enhancing Performance: Unleashing Your True Potential (Bundled)

Innovations in Mind/Body Therapies

The Mind/Body Connection

The New Biology

The Neurology of Mind/Body Health

Transformation Revisited

The Immune System Primer

Using Imagery to Heal

A Quick Pain Management Primer

Healing the Body Basics

The Mind, Surgery, and Recovery

Calming Your Gut

Innovations in Mind/Body Therapies (Bundled)

The Neurology of Suggestion Series

The Neurology of Suggestion

Advanced Hypnotherapy Protocols and Applications

The Neurology of Suggestion Series (Bundled)

The Neurology of Suggestion Basics

Change: A New Paradigm for Transformation

Brain Potential: Enhancing and Inhibiting for Peak Performance

Reshaping: Changing your Brain and Body

Mastering Change: 10 Principles for Transformation

Achieving Lasting Change: A System for Transformation

Neurology of Suggestion Applications

The Neurology of Suggestion Basics (Bundled)

Neuro Linguistic Programming Basics

Mastering the NLP Communication Model

Developing Instant Rapport

The Basis of NLP Techniques

Modeling Behavior

Practical NLP Applications

Neuro Linguistic Programming Basics (Bundled)

Individual Books

Advanced Hypnotherapy Script Writing Techniques

Clinical Hypnotherapy Fundamentals

Healing the Body

Healing the Mind

New Directions in Hypnotherapy

Rapid Change: The Secrets of Lasting Personal and Group Transformation

Space/Time-based Interventions: Simple techniques that enhance hypnotherapy

www.ingramcontent.com/pod-product-compliance
Lightning Source LLC
Chambersburg PA
CBHW072251260726
48657CB00005BA/2205